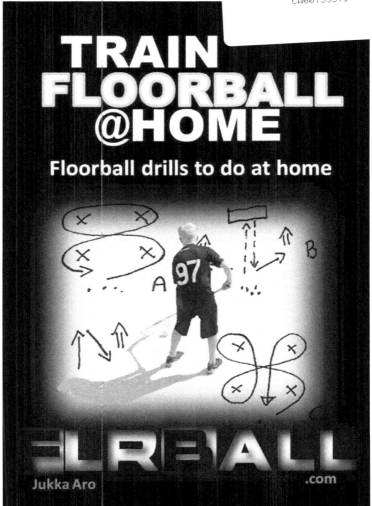

TRAIN FLOORBALL @HOME

Floorball drills to do at home

FLRBALL .com

Jukka Aro

Förlag: BoD – Books on Demand, Stockholm, Sverige
Tryck: BoD – Books on Demand, Norderstedt, Tyskland
ISBN: 978-91-7851-249-2

Content

Practice Floorball at Home

READ THIS FIRST

The book has "many" pages, but the first 50 pages are more text-rich and pages where I want to convey knowledge and tips to you as a floorball player, things that are good to know and to think about.

Invest the time to read through the first chapters (about 50 pages), read by yourself or together with a parent (if you are a younger player). The text is "simple" and with large text, you can do it!

I am confident that you will find great tips and thoughtful things on those pages, which will also help you develop, as a floorball player, and help you as you begin to look at the drills later in the book.

I wish you nice reading ☺

Practice Floorball at Home

Practicing floorball at home or having your own drive (motivation) to practice at home in addition to team training is one of the best qualities a floorball player can have and a master key to success.

It is not always, or it will not always be fun to train yourself, but if you make it a routine and a good habit, then the results will come and it will be fun to play floorball, all training is useful and something which you will benefit from!

The better you are at something, the more fun it will be, your own training will help you along that path.

Make the exercise a daily good habit, which you do in the long term, you will not be the best, because you are practicing today and not because you are training tomorrow, but you will be good or even maybe the best, because you can keep training for a long period of time and train extra on your own!

... Right now, I'm being interrupted by an 11-year-old who asks, "Can I do some "physics", or do I disturb you in your writing?"

"Of course you can train, you will not disturb and you don't have to ask for permission to do that" ☺

In the book you will get a lot of tips on practices with stick and ball, but also physical and coordination training, which you can easily do yourself at home (indoors or outdoors).

The exercises with stick, ball and shots could require some kind of surface to be on, in order to protect the floor or if you are outdoors or in the garage or some similar space, to protect the stick and give you good surface to practice on. You will get some tips on the surfaces that you can use, for the skill drills later in the book.

Depending on the space, if you skip the shots, the drills can actually be carried out inside your room as well in a very limited space.

Before we go into the drills, we will briefly look at what is required, to succeed as a floorball player and some tips on practice equipment, surfaces to practice on and on other things you can think of, such as rest, diet and having good routines.

Invest your time in reading through these pages, I am convinced that the pages help you as a floorball player, but also in other areas, the word floorball, can be exchanged for school or other sports, the same principles apply there to succeed.

What is required to succeed in floorball?

10,000 repetitions / hours

What does it take to succeed or become really good at floorball? A number of studies have shown that it takes tens of thousands of hours to become a master of what you do.

Each of us has the potential to be a "champion" in what we do, but it will take time, specifically 10,000 hours of good training or about ten years, which is also why I wrote in the introduction that you will not be best because you practice today, but if you do it day after day or at least very frequently, then you will be good in the long run, just practice a lot on your own and can keep up the training over time.

The same way of thinking can be used, for example, in skills training, for a movement (fake as an example) to be automated, you need to have about 10,000 repetitions, that is to repeat the movement 10,000 times for it to be smooth and automated ("you know when it goes by itself ").

If you were to do a toe drag 100 times a day, you need to do it for 100 days, to get a really good at it and reach up to 10,000 times. If you do it 20 times a day, it will take 500 days or about a year and a half to get really good at it.

Since I gave you example of how long it takes to "automate" a "toe drag", we can also look at what 10,000 hours of training means.

In order to reach 10,000 hours you need to practice in a good way (properly), this is not only about training floorball (of course), but more about as I wrote before, all training is good training and hours that you get into your "training account".

To get up to 10,000 hours in 10 years, you need to practice 20 hours a week. Then it might be better to talk about physically activated (school sports, team training, training on your own, games and activities with friends, street floorball, paddle, tennis, golf, hockey, soccer, running, cycling, etc.)

Training versatility makes it easier and maybe even more fun to collect the training hours in to the "10,000 hours - training account"?

Here it might also be important to show an opposite example, if you, on the other hand, only practice with your own team, 2-3 times a week + some school sports and thus land on 4-5 activity hours per week and the rest of the time, 5-6 hours a day is used for Fortnite or other console games and mobile, it will take you almost 40 years to reach up to 10,000 hours and become really good at floorball!

On the other hand, you will be really good at Fortnite within 5 years!

After 5 years you are up to 10,000 hours with 6 hours of Fortnite per day!

Conversely, if you use Fortnite time for training and practice as much as in the game example with Fortnite, you would be really awesome in floorball within 5 years!

Remember, all training is good training, which develops you and which you will have with you!

A talent or someone who has trained a lot?

Talent is surely a word that you have heard said many times about some players or maybe even about yourself?

Unfortunately, talent is not such a good word (explain soon) and is about a "locked or closed mindset" when you say someone has talent, it is in some way, whether you either "got it" or "didn't get it" ", you either got it or you were left without it.

Or that you do not need or did not need to train as hard as everyone else, you are a talent. We can have different traits for different things and of course there is something about, what we have inherited from our parents and grandparents.

You may have gifted parents, but is it probably more realistic that parents have also put a lot of effort into training themselves, once upon a time?

They also have a better feeling, knowledge and understanding, of what it takes to be good in form of training and can convey this and coach their children.

Of course, the knowledge that experienced parents can convey can be acquired in other ways as well. You can access some of that knowledge by reading this book.

What if it wasn't, that "talent is innate", and it can only be seen as a statement that diminishes our belief that we can be the best, or creates a false sense of security, I'm a talent, I don't have to work as hard as the others?

What happens if our success is only linked to how many hours we practice and the most important factor is your own drive (motivation) to practice?

Tiger Woods, a golf talent? Or a lot of training?

You know who Tiger Woods is? He is perhaps the greatest golf star ever?

Tiger Woods has also been seen as the greatest "talent" in golf ever. Is he really a "talent" who has received "everything for free" and just "grown up to a superstar"? Or how is it?

The truth is that Tiger Woods got his first golf set before he was **one year old**!

He had gone through his first full golf round at the **age of two**.

By the time he was **five**, he had already **trained more** than an average golfer will do throughout his career!

As a **five-year-old**, he had **trained more** than most adults! So it is definitely **more about training than "innate talent"**.

The same goes for Galante, Kohonen, Kauppi, Messi, Beckham, Ronaldo, Forsberg, Gretzky, Crosby, McDavid and the other sport superstars, a huge number of training hours are behind the success.

"With hard work everything is possible, everyone can dream, what you dream of you can achieve, if you are willing to work for it" / Lionel Messi, soccer player

If we take an ice hockey example, during the summer you can read and see pictures in the newspapers and online, "NHL players on holiday", "NHL stars relaxing" and " NHL players enjoying their holidays". Is it just that they "relax" and take it easy, during the summer?
It is at least easy to get that picture reading the news.

No, of course it's not true, the reality is that they train 5-10 times a week during their "vacation", some of the players train even more.

Even though they are big stars, they need to train to keep their level and get better, the same goes for all of us, no matter what level we play or what sport we are involved in.

The belief that talent and talent are somewhat innate is strong in many individuals and parents, but more and more research show that genes have a very small, if at all, role for "talent". Instead, **training**, **encouragement** and **motivation (self-driven)** are lifted as the most crucial for success!

When football coach José Mourinho came to Real Madrid he commented on Christiano Ronaldo (who played there then): *"He works extremely hard, it is impressive to see a player of his caliber (who is so good), who trains harder than anyone else".*

If you count the hours the "stars" have spent on training, it wouldn't be a surprise why they are there, where they are and of course, it's not just about sport-specific training (Sport-specific, for example, just practicing floorball).

"Practicing is my secret, I have always believed that if you want to be successful you have to work for it, train and practice and practice more". / David Beckham, soccer player

The same is true in for floorball success, training and practicing, repeating, repeating, practicing and training.

Automated movements will build your capacity and help you take the next step in your development.

It's kind of like learning to ride a bike, once you've "automated" it (learned), it will sit in the spinal cord, you may not be a master cyclist, but you will master the technique and balance and can take the next developmental step (e.g. releasing the handlebars with one hand). The basic skill is always there even after 40 years.

This may be a bit of a premium (extra knowledge), but there is a theory called the Pareto Rule 20-80.

The 20/80 rule says that, 80% of your results will come from 20% of your activities / practices / skills, to put it simply you can say that, if there is, let's say 20 fakes, then the four fakes that you master well and use, gives you success 8 out of 10 times. In other words, it is not the number of different fakes for example, that makes you good.

Once you have automated a basic skill at the bottom, it is easy to "spontaneously" add a moment e.g. during a match.

What I want to say is that, you do not have to be a champion and master 100 different fakes, choose some that you become "master" of, and that become your own "special moves".

These will already give you good results and a base to tap into other skills, other "skills" that you have trained to be proficient at.

If we take the example of the toe drag, when you have also trained a lot of shots and automated the shooting movement (you do not have to think about it when you do it, 10,000 repetitions), and if you have practiced the toe drag 100 times a day for 100 days (10,000 repetitions), you will be able to combine these two and get really good effect from them, who isn't fooled by a shot fake, followed by a toe drag, which ends with a fast and precise shot?

Two steps that you are the master of and can link to other tricks and shots.

You can see incredible fakes and things being done by the stars in the highest floorball leagues and for that matter at the absolute highest speed, and we, or many of those watching are surprised, how did they succeed or how could he do it?

The answer is simple, through repetition, repetition and hours of training, to automate the movements! It is then, "it just comes by itself"

Another way of finding "talents" or good hockey players…

Many floorball and hockey coaches talk about finding and seeing talents, is it true? Or are they just good at seeing and spotting players who have already trained more than the others at a certain age? Or do they have other tricks to spot good players?

Let's take one more example from hockey…

Teemu Selanne (perhaps Finland's best ice hockey player, who has, among other things, the Rookie record in the NHL), talked about success and talent at his hockey camp in Vuokatti, Finland.

Teemu Selanne told about a team selection in Russia, where the legendary Russian coach and player Tarasov would put together an elite group of ten-year old hockey players.

When the players arrived at the arena, he divided the players into teams outside the locker room, you can go into that locker room, you can go to the other and so on.

Then he stated that the first sorting was done, and that one team will win big!

An assistant coach asked him, how he could be so sure about that?

Tarasov replied that he would see it during the match, but he himself was 100% sure that the team he had chosen would win.

Very well, the team that Tarasov had chosen and pointed out as the winners won the game, they actually won the match by 12-2!

How could he see the talent or how good the players were without having seen the players in the rink or even dressed up with the equipment?

The secret was that he put all the players whose mum or dad carried the hockey equipment (bag and sticks) for, in one locker room and all the players, who came and carried their equipment themselves in the other.

To be clear, it was the team of players who carried their own equipment, the team that Tarasov believed in as the winners.

How could it be crucial for the outcome of the match, to carry their own bag?

He looked at the players drive and motivation, players who carry their own equipment are also probably players, who can go out and train extra themselves, get to the training area nearby, the running track, the gym, or the skill / shooting pad at home.

Simple isn't it? Carrying your own equipment is also good training in itself, even if the floorball equipment weighs a lot less than hockey equipment.

Your own drive to train, is a success factor! Take responsibility for your own development!

How have today's floorball stars reached the top?

Everyone has:
Started their career early, around the age of 5-6. (But remember what I've written before, it's about getting together the training hours, if you start later, you have to train even more on your own).

Been very physically active and engaged in many sports during growing up, although floorball may have always been number one.

At the age of 10-11, they have trained (been physically active) around 20-30 hours a week, where the greatest amount or number of hours have come from spontaneous training (trained themselves and played / trained with friends).

Enjoyed good training opportunities (close by).

Trained and played with older players, much here in the form of spontaneous sports on the street or an area nearby.

Had support from parents and help of "enthusiasts" in the floorball organization, for extra training.

Living with orderly conditions, focusing on order and good routines, with food, sleep and priority on sports.

You have to have the aptitude for different things, but it is still **your own drive / motivation** (love what you do) that is number one, then it is also easy to get together **the training hours**, which are required to succeed!

Practice at home vs team practice

Training vs Match vs Training at home

What gives you the most development as a player, match or practice? Or how much does it give you to practice at home? If we only think about developing you as an individual, where are you able to develop most, and train most effectively?

If we look at some figures from matches and training sessions, you will have the answer to what is best, with regard to the development of you as a player.

A floorball match in numbers:

The following statistics symbolize a floorball match that takes not more than 60 minutes to complete (2x20 min = 50-60 min)

• A floorball player will have the ball on the blade for <u>an average</u> of **8 seconds** per player and match.

• A floorball player takes on average **1 - 2 shots** per match.

• **99% of the feedback** and **comments** from the coaches happen to the players when they have the ball. Ironically, floorball players only have the **ball on their stick** for 0.2% of the time in a floorball game.

On a floorball practice (Team training):

On a floorball practice, the player has the ball on the blade between **5-10 minutes** and shoots between **20-30 shots.**

Many times, the active part during a practice is anything between **8-30 minutes** of effective time (when the player is active and not waiting for his turn, listening to the coach, moving balls / shooting balls to the boards, etc.).

A practice at home

How does it look like if you practice at home yourself? How much do you need to train?

The effect of a shot / skill pad at home is great, and you are surprised of how much you can work out and repeat different parts in a very short time, which nevertheless corresponds to more than an extra team training.

A team training, which you get together 20-30 shots, on a 60-minute floorball training, or ball on the blade for 5-10 minutes.

Then you can easily shoot 50 shots in about 10 minutes on the shooting pad at home (little bit depending on how many floorball's you have available). Or if you dribble with a ball for 10 minutes, you have had the ball on the blade for as long as on a regular practice (this for a maximum investment of 20 minutes of your time).

In 30 minutes you can fire away 100 shots and dribble with ball on the blade for 10-15 minutes!

30 minutes each day is not a huge amount of time to invest in yourself to become a better floorball player.

Just think about how much time you spend on your cellphone or Xbox / PlayStation every day (surveys show anything between 2-7 hours a day). How does it look like for you?

Later in the book, there are also tips on how to put together a physics/strength practice for yourself, which also takes no more than 30 minutes to complete.

Shot and skill practice at home gives a tremendous effect, if you have the possibility and motivation to do it.

Floorball matches are fun and definitely needed, this is where you and your teammates can see the effect of the training.

Of course, team training is also hugely important, floorball is a team sport and we should train together, but as an **individual** you can develop yourself very much on your own, train yourself or with friends at home, and you will see a wonderful development over time!

Be long-term and keep practicing!

Eat and sleep correctly and have routines

Eat and sleep correctly and have routines

The heading contains three important ingredients in addition to the training itself, for a floorball player or any athlete.

All the parts, training, recovery (sleep) and diet (food) need to be in balance with each other, in order for you to develop and utilize the training in the best way and to avoid overload, illnesses and injuries.

If you also have routines for sleep, food and training, then you have really good conditions for success (Routines - habit of doing things at certain times or in certain order)

Good habits and routines

Being a floorball player is all about thinking the whole picture (holistic view), you are not just a floorball player during a training or the match.

- Rest and sleep are extremely important in order to accommodate your practice, stick to regular sleep times, try to sleep and wake up at the same time every day, your body and brain will enjoy it.

- Good and nutritious food throughout the day, at the right interval.

This requires planning and maybe some help from the parents. Eat properly every time, the food is not always good, but you need the nutrition!

- Create routines for the training, by finding times (e.g. at 4pm right after school I train myself) or arranging activities that you do every day. When you get home,

1. Do your homework
2. Practice extra yourself
3. Eat food
4. Play Xbox
5. Go to the team training
6. Eat food…

Repeat the same sequence every day, some days may not have all the activities (you may not have homework every day and not the team training either), but think in that order, or create your own order, that you write down and visualize for yourself.

Very few and simple tips, which give you the opportunity to develop even more and take full advantage of the effect of the training and by doing it this way it simply becomes a routine or habit, a good habit.

Stick to your routines, in order to make it a good habit!

Regular circadian rhythm

Outside of sports, the daily rhythm is one of the most important areas, together with regular food intake.

A night's poor sleep does not do much, but a growing lack of sleep will affect, responsiveness, reflexes, memory functions and increase the risk of infection (the risk of getting sick – if you are often sick, you can think about if you sleep enough and if you eat enough and varied nutritious food).

In order to perform at the top and develop as an athlete, the daily rhythm should be the same throughout the week, an hour here or there will not hurt, but disturbances of three hours and over will affect the "biological clock" in your body, at worst, you might have got Jet-lag symptoms (more on this on the next page).

The recommended amount of sleep for young players is approx. 9 to 10 hours of sleep per night.

Jet-lag among athletic youth

I wrote about Jet-lag symptoms on the previous page, what is it then?

You can be affected by Jet-lag symptoms if you travel over several time zones (east to west or west to east) and have to adapt to a new circadian rhythm, it is not just to change the daily rhythm by a button push for the body and mind, this will not happen over a day or a night.

So if you travel to another time zone (USA / Asia / Europe) you can get something called "Jet-lag" symptoms, you feel tired, powerless / lack of energy and are awake when you should sleep and would like to sleep when you are awake .

Many or most serious athletic youths manage their rest and sleep quite correctly during the weeks, but during the weekends when there is extra time for recovery, many of the athletes turn around the clock and use the nights for e.g. to play Fortnite or other console games, far too long into the small hours.

To put it simply, you are in the US and in their time zone even though you are at home in Europe! Or in US moving from East coast time zone to West coast time zone.

"Turning around the clock" like in the example, means that in the coming week, when it is time to train hard again, you suffer from a self-created Jet-lag (lack of energy), which affects the whole week's practices and matches, you feel tired and powerless and cannot perform your best neither on training nor on match.

A good benchmark is that your body can adapt **one hour per day**, to "turn the clock" with 5-6 hours during the weekend, will create problems throughout the coming week, on Friday your body has recovered from the time shift, and then it is weekend again...

In a study on the oldest boy team players and juniors in Jyvaskyla, Finland. Most of the players showed burnout syndromes, when they returned after the summer break and it was not because they had trained too much (physically).

The researchers found that the symptoms could be linked to poor sleep.

The bad sleep could be linked to shift of circadian rhythm, and games like Fortnite / CS / GTA, which are very intense for the brain, the games affect sleep even if some of the players went to bed in a "reasonable time", but the brain was still at full speed after all gaming and affected the sleep. Something to consider?

I'm not against console games, it's just about finding a good balance for you, between sleep - food - training and Xbox.

Games like Fortnite or different sport games are good for developing the brain, for training the brain to process a lot of information, make quick decisions, collaborate and communicate with friends, like in real life floorball, but keep in mind your sleep, and the fact that gaming does not take away your own training time at home.

It is good to switch off the game a while before you go to bed to let the brain "cool down" so that you can sleep better.

Training surfaces

Training surfaces

To be able to practice stickhandling or shots, you might need some kind of surface to practice on, or if some marks are okay on the floor, you practice on that! Below are although some suggestions and different alternatives, which work for that purpose (protect the floor, your stick and give you good surface to practice on).

Search the web for places to buy and for price (Enter floorball shooting pad, floorball skill pad or floorball skill zone in Google). Some proposals will come from hockey, but these surfaces are good and will work for your floorball practice.

 A small shooting pad, for shots and smaller skill drills. However, this size will be too small <u>for many</u> of the skill drills in the book. But works well for pure shot training.

A larger skill and shooting pad that will work for all the drills in the book. (Designed originally for hockey)

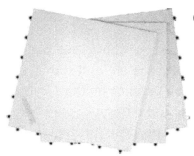

Or build a skill pad / shooting pad of your own size with smaller tiles that you pinch together, works for both skills training and shots.

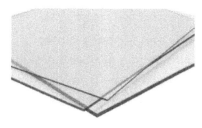

Other alternatives to shot and skill training can be found e.g. at Do It Yourself shops (DIY), "plexiglass screens" that will work for shots and smaller skill

training.

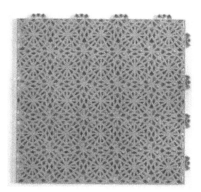

DIY or similar stores have tiles that you can also build to any size and color. Perfect surface for training of shots and skill training.

IKEA also has an alternative for skill training and shooting, the floor protection cover KOLON. If you want to get away cheaply, then this is the cheapest option, approx. 20-25 Euros € / Dollars $ / Pounds £.

Works for shots and skill training.

Training equipment

Training equipment

To make the skill training more fun and challenging, we can look at some things you can use. There is much to build or buy, but we will take the most important and the slightly cheaper variants.

Cones or hockey pucks (sometimes cheaper than the cones) to dribble around and past are good to have.

Personally I use broken hockey stick shafts (lightweight) as obstacles, these can usually be found in special "trashcans" in a hockey arena, perfect to jump over, flip the ball over, run a long drag in between, fake shots at, protect the ball at, etc.

Or take a shaft from a brush or rake, it will fulfill the same function.

Three hockey pucks or wooden blocks under the shaft at each end provide the opportunity to pull the ball under or act as a jumping obstacle.

All of these training tools and steps provide an extra challenge and at the same time reduce the time to perform the next step (match-like) without having "real" opponents.

The last tip is a ball passer, if you can't get the siblings or parents to act as a passers...

A **car tire** also works as a passer or a **wooden plank**...

The last tip is a safety net for the balls, I myself have bought a load net for trailer 3.5 m x 2.5 m, much cheaper than all other variants and fulfills its function.

Trailer loading net suspended behind the target, as a safety net.

Compete – Train Match-like

Compete and challenge yourself

Do you remember the 10,000 training hours, which are effective and challenging, or the 10,000 repetitions needed to become good or to automate a movement?

To make the training challenging, exciting and to be able to exercise and find it fun to practice, it can be good to try to compete against yourself and beat different own records.

How many shots out of 10 do you put in a certain place e.g. right top corner?

How many shots do you need to hit 5 times at a certain spot in the goal / net?

Start the timer on your cellphone and take time on how long it takes to hit a certain place in the goal 5 times.

How many repetitions do you manage to do in 30 seconds / 60 seconds? (Dribble an 8, toe drags, backhand toe drags etc.)

How many times in a row do you manage to hit the right top corner, for example?

Set order for the shots, the first shot should be at the left post low, the next in the left top corner, the right post low, the right top corner and finally in the middle low, how many balls did you need? Or how far did you come with 10 balls? Or how long time did it take?

It can also be motivating to <u>write down your records</u> and dates when you made them.

First of all, you will remember them and you will see how much you develop over time and it will be a challenge for you to beat your own records.

You can also keep track of <u>how many days</u> you have been training or how long you have been training, you will find some tables at the end of the book, which you can use for this purpose ...or create your own.

Below is an example where you can keep track of how many times you have e.g. practiced 100 shots or practiced on a certain fake 100 times - 100 days.

100 days X 100 times = 10,000 repetitions!

100 Day Challenge									
Activity:									
1	2	3	4	5	6	7	8	9	10
11	12	13	14	15	16	17	18	19	20
21	22	23	24	25	26	27	28	29	30
31	32	33	34	35	36	37	38	39	40
41	42	43	44	45	46	47	48	49	50
51	52	53	54	55	56	57	58	59	60
61	62	63	64	65	66	67	68	69	70
71	72	73	74	75	76	77	78	79	80
81	82	83	84	85	86	87	88	89	90
91	92	93	94	95	96	97	98	99	100

This table and some others are at the end of the book.

There are some physical exercises later in the book, these you can also mix in, before and between shot and skill training.

With the physical exercises you raise your pulse and it becomes more like a match, you will be a little "breathless" and with higher pulse, when you get the shot opportunity (take the shot), match-like and a little harder to get the precision of the shots.

You will quickly get better and above all a better goal scorer on the matches with this set up, a little pulse and fatigue will not disturb you at the moment of shooting in a real game!

Drawing explanations

Drawing explantions

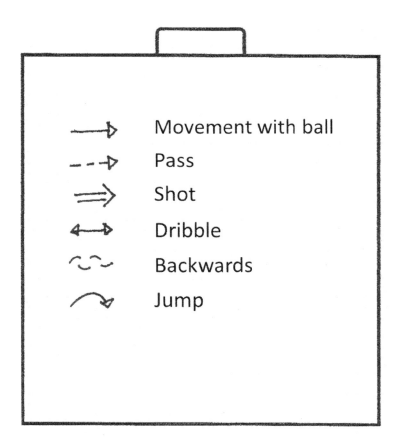

Symbol	Meaning
→	Movement with ball
- - -↣	Pass
⇒	Shot
↤—↦	Dribble
⌒⌒	Backwards
⌒↘	Jump

Drawing explantions

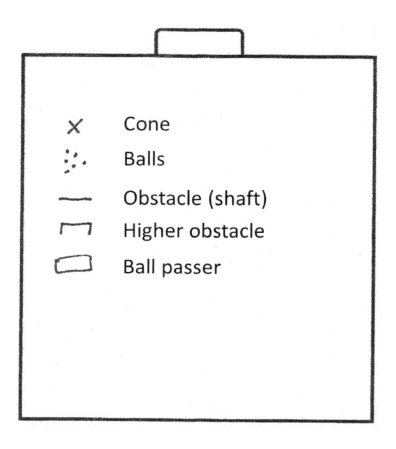

✕	Cone
∴	Balls
—	Obstacle (shaft)
⊓	Higher obstacle
▭	Ball passer

Below are some explanatory pictures of the fakes and dekes that come later in the book.

Toe-drag
(Pull the ball back with the tip of the blade)

Backhand toe drag
(Toe-drag on the backhand side - sideways)

Backhand pull or toe drag
(Move forward and then pull back the ball)

Shooting drills

Shooting drills

The first shooting drills are more about getting together a good amount of shots (amount training). Focus on shooting quickly and unannounced (don't dribble the ball a few times before shooting).

You can also practice hiding where the shot is coming, sending incorrect information about where you intend to shoot to the goalkeeper.

You can do this by, for example, looking left and shooting right, or tilting the blade and hands slightly to the left, but right at the moment of shooting you turn the shot to the right. Hard or at least much harder for the goalkeepers to save the shot.

Instead of just taking a ball and shooting, you can also kick the ball to the blade and shoot as fast as possible.

Use different shooting techniques and shoot both forehand and backhand shots.

You can also vary the position of how and where you stand, practice shooting from uncomfortable positions and strange angles as well.

You can also add steps from the chapter jumps and steps in to the shooting drills.

A few steps sideways back and forth or jump over an obstacle before a shot, and you practice coordination, physics and shots.

In some cases the drills are drawn and the descriptions, to keep the stick "Left". If you are instead playing "Right", you may need to mirror some of the drills later in the book.

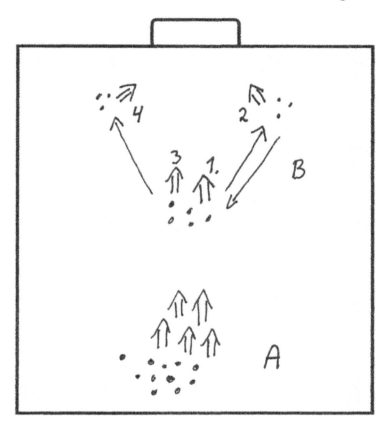

A: Gather the balls and shoot! Get as many shots together as possible, shoot quickly and without dribbling. Shoot with different techniques (wrist shot, slap shot, backhand, etc.) Vary the position of the balls.

B: Shoot from center, to the side for a rebound shot, back to center for shot, to the side for a rebound.

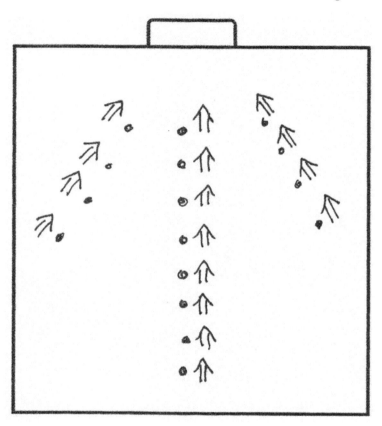

Line up the balls and shoot one by one, aiming at the same spot in the goal to get the feeling for the shot from different distances.

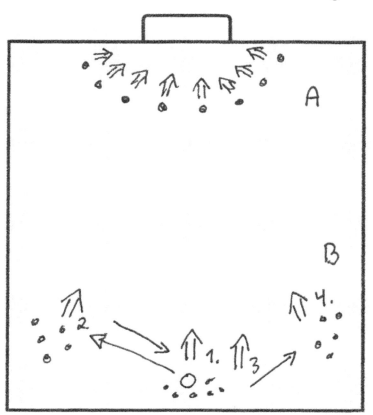

A: Close shots with balls lined up in a crescent.

B: Shot from middle, to the side for an angle shot.

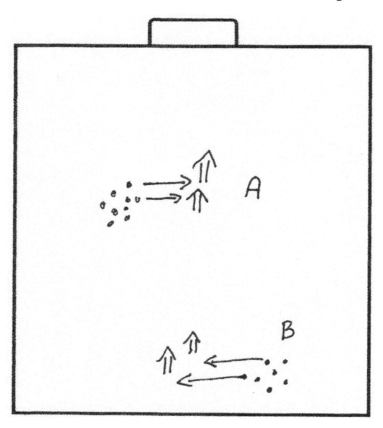

A: Pull the ball towards you (toe drag) and shoot in the same motion.

B: Pull the ball with the backhand and shoot forehand in one motion.

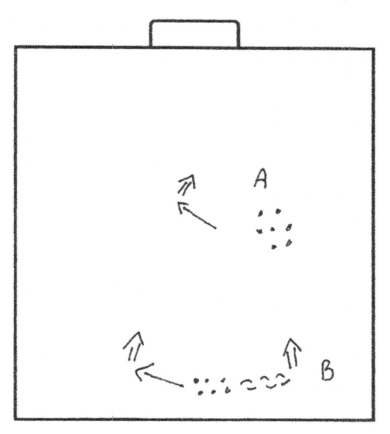

A: Move the ball diagonally to the left, look at the left side, wiggle your hands so that it seems like you are going to shoot left. At the moment of shooting, you angle to the right instead.

B: Take a ball from the center and move it sideways, forwards and backwards before shooting.

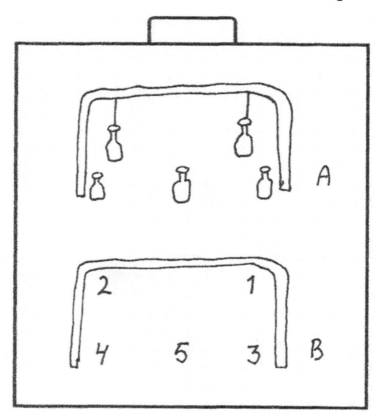

A: Energize the shooting practice with some targets to aim for. Use PET-bottles with some water in and put or hang in strategic places in the goal.

B: Set an order for how to shoot.

Shots with obstacles

Shots with obstacles

Shots with obstacle add extra dimension to the shooting moment and you get the feeling of moving the ball sideways just before the shot, making it harder for the goalkeepers to save your shot.

An obstacle can be a shaft, some cones or a leftover chair that you can dribble sideways and shoot past, just like in a match with a defender in front of you.

An old chair can act as a defender, shoot past or "between the legs on the defender", challenging.

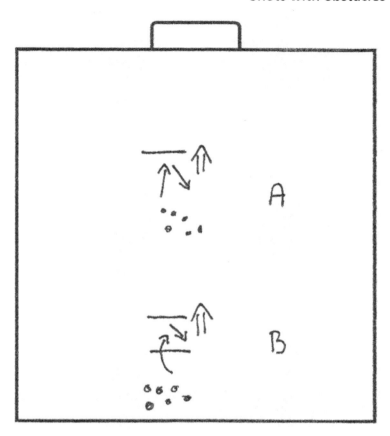

A: Move the ball towards the obstacle and then back before shooting (backhand pull or toe drag)

B: Flip the ball over the first obstacle (or raise the obstacle and place the ball under), backhand pull or toe drag fake before shooting.

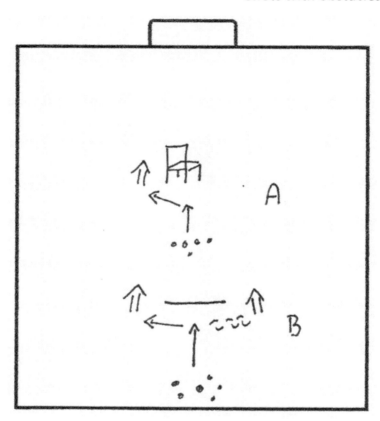

A: Move the ball toward the obstacle and to the side before shooting. Depending on the type of chair you have, you can also practice shooting a low shot between the defender's legs (the chairs).

B: Move the ball toward the obstacle and aside before shooting. (Forward in one direction, backwards in the other)

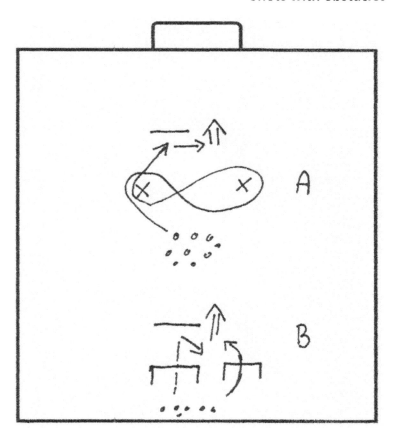

A: Dribble in an 8th, backhand toe or toe drag at the obstacle before the shot.

B: Punch the ball under one obstacle and jump over the other yourself, pulling the ball back at the obstacle before shooting (backhand pull or toe drag).

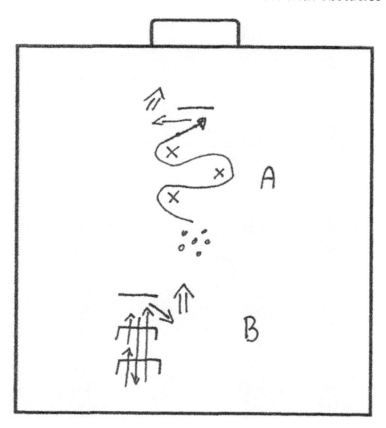

A: Slalom past the cones, longer lateral pull before the shot. B: Punch the ball under the first obstacle and stop it before the second, then pull the ball under the second obstacle, back to the starting position with a long pull and back to the obstacle at the front again, backhand pull or toe drag and shot.

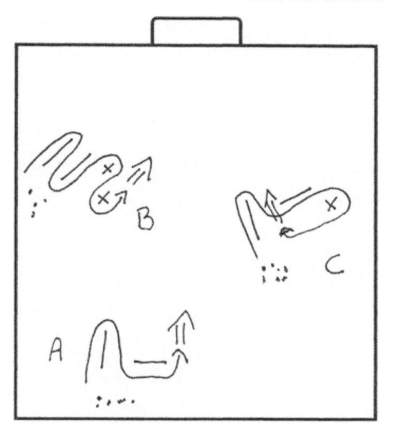

A: Long pull forward, toe drag back, long sideways movement before shot.

B: Long pull forward, toe drag back, long pull forward, and toe drag back in slalom and shot in one motion.

C: Long pull forward, toe drag back and sideways around the cone, shot.

Skill tracks

Skill tracks

Depending on where you are (outdoors / indoors) and the size of your surface, the skill tracks can be performed with or without shots.

Practice on quick soft movements and many repetitions of the movements.

In the case of fake, it is always good to "exaggerate" the movement, so that the opponent is really convinced about the fake.

If you end with a shot, think of the tips from the shot section

Focus on shooting quickly and precise.

You can also practice hiding where the shot is coming (send incorrect information about where you intend to shoot to the goalkeeper).

Use different shooting techniques and shoot both forehand and backhand shots.

You can also vary how you stand, practice shooting from uncomfortable positions as well.

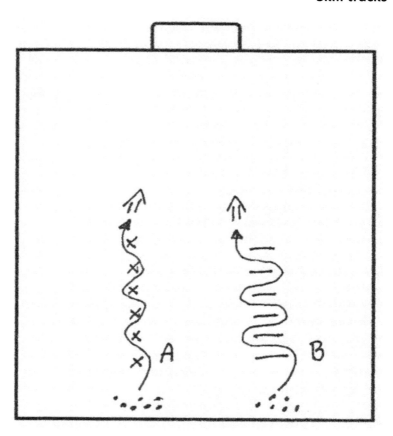

A: Fast short draws and shot.

B: Longer pulls past stick shaft and shot.

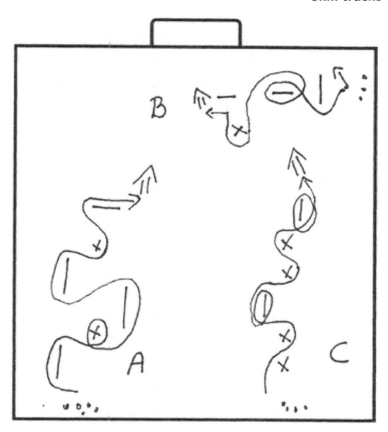

A: Long forward movement, around the cone, long forward x 2, around the cone, long lateral movement and shot without hitting the obstacle behind the blade.
B: Start with a fake, step aside, longer draw around the next obstacle, around the cone, small sideways movement and shot. C: Slalom between the cones, longer full turns around the shafts on the sides, shot.

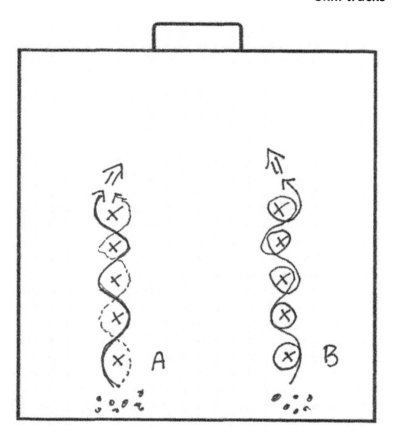

A: Ball on one side body on other (quick short steps), shot.

B: Full lap with ball around the cones, shot.

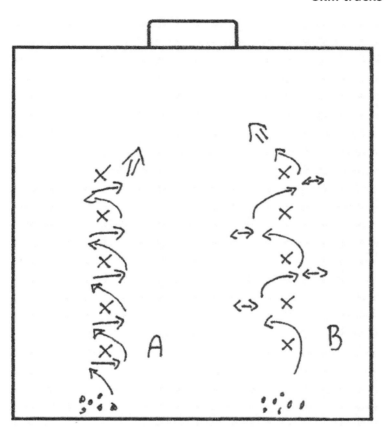

A: Toe drags or backhand toe drags between the cones, before shooting.

B: Slalom between the cones, with a few short dribbles on the side after each cone, finish with shot.

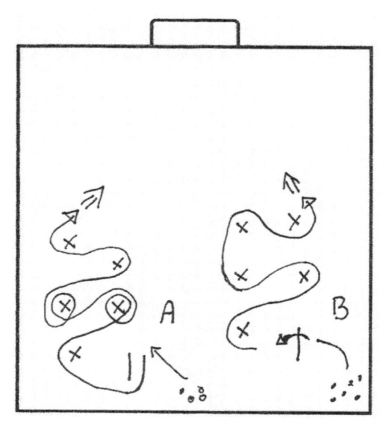

A: Long pull aside at the shaft, around the cone, full lap around the next two cones, and slalom before shot.

B: Flip the ball over the first obstacle, slalom between the cones, shot.

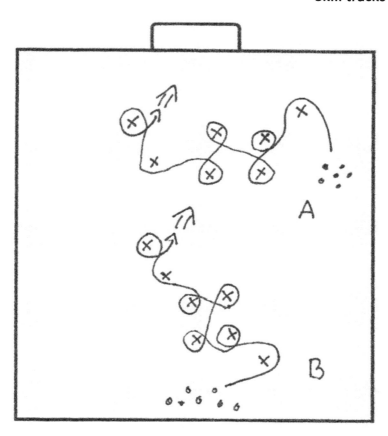

A: Around the first cone, full lap around the next four cones, past the sixth cone, full lap around the last cone before the shot.

B: Same drill as A, but instead of sideways, you can run the drill straight towards the goal.

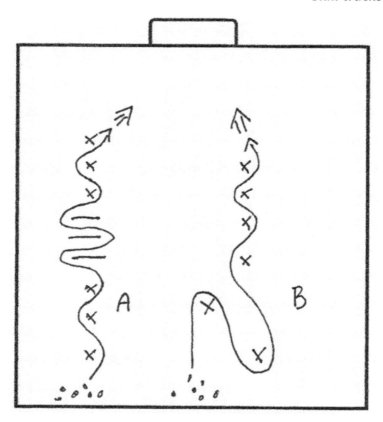

A: Slalom with short quick draws, longer draws at the stick shafts, short quick draws again before shooting.

B: Long diagonal draw, before short fast draws and shot.

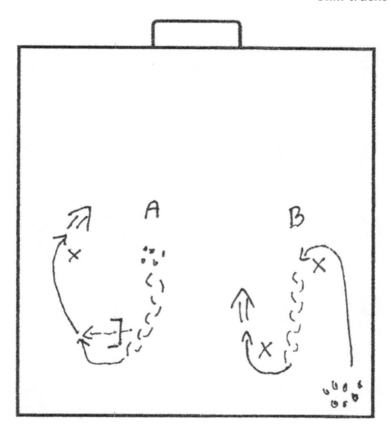

A: Back with the ball against the obstacle, poke the ball under, round the cone before an angle shot.

B: Forward with the ball, back up, turn at the cone (facing the cone) and finish. You can also practice turning with your back towards the cone.

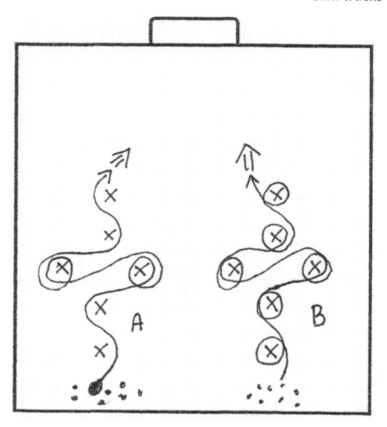

A: Slalom with full lap around the cones in the middle.

B: Same path as A, but full lap around each cone.

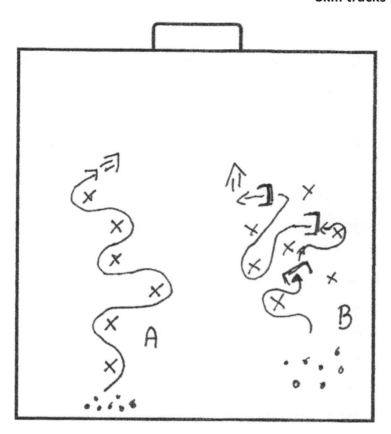

A: Slalom between the cones, the cone in the middle and the last cone further out for a longer pull.

B: Spread out obstacles and cones and dribble creatively in any path before shooting.

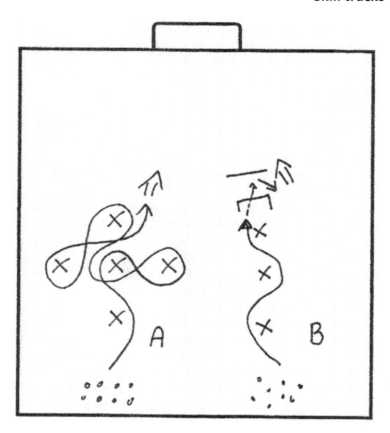

A: Dribble towards the cone in the middle, out to the right, back to the middle, the cone at the front, to the left, shot.

B: Slalom past the cones, pass the ball under the obstacle, pull it aside or back at the next obstacle, shot.

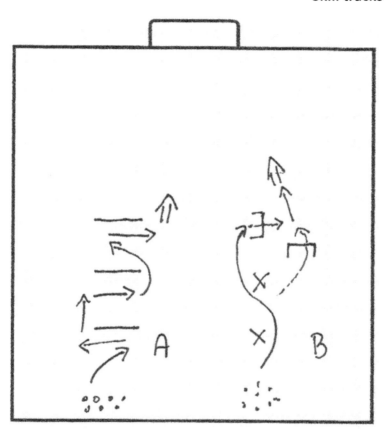

A: Angle body and ball to the right, go left, backhand toe at the next obstacle, go left pull right at the last obstacle before shooting.

B: Slalom between the cones, jump one obstacle yourself and poke the ball under the other, shot.

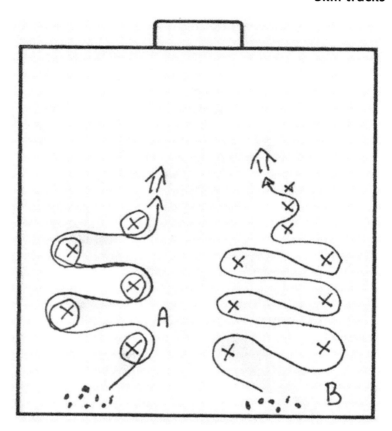

A: Full lap around the cones on the track, shot.

B: Long and slightly diagonal draws backwards in the first part, short quick draws before the shot.

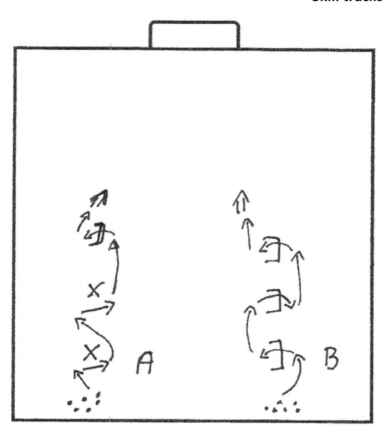

A: Toe-drag or backhand-toe drag at the first obstacles, flipping the ball or jumping over the last obstacle before shooting.

B: Jump over the obstacles and move the ball in front of the obstacle or flip over the ball and jump yourself, shot.

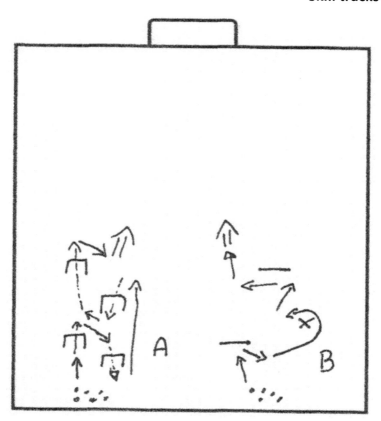

A: Punch the ball under the first two obstacles, short fast moves, push the ball forward and back under the next obstacle, under the last obstacle before the shot.

B: Start with a backhand pull or toe drag fake at the first obstacle, around the cone, long sideways draw at the last obstacle and shot.

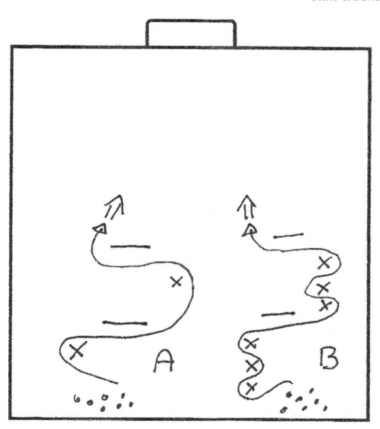

A: Take the ball around the cone and past the obstacle X 2, shot. (Keep body far away when you pull the ball around the cone, only the blade and the ball go around the cone).

B: Short fast slalom, long sideways draw, short fast draws, long sideways draw and shot.

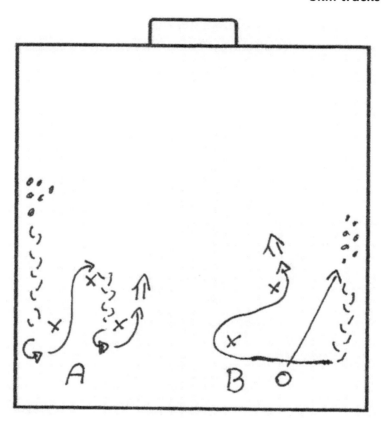

A: Dribble the ball backwards towards the cone, do a backward turn facing away from the cone, move the ball forward and backwards again with a backward turn at the last cone, shot.

B: Run to the ball, backwards with the ball, slalom between the cones, shot.

Stickhandling and fakes on small surface

Stickhandling and fakes on a small surface

These drills easily become "stationary" if you do not think of moving your feet as well.

Practice moving your feet's and center of gravity in these drills.

When it comes to your feet's, you can

- Run on the spot
- Move sideways, back and forth
- Move forward and backward
- Stand on one leg
- Jump on the spot
- Jump on one leg
- - Work with the center of gravity, move it from right to left.

You also have suggestions later in the book during the chapter Jumps and Steps, link these movements to the drills in this chapter.

Stickhandling and fakes on a small surface

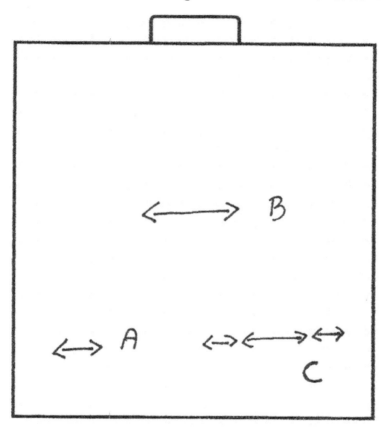

A: Dribble short quick

B: Long draws

C: Short dribble in outer positions, long pull to change sides.

Stickhandling and fakes on a small surface

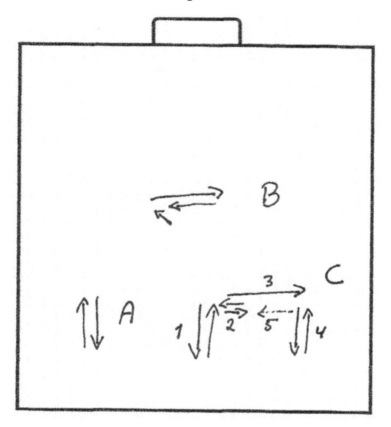

A: Toe-drags

B: Backhandtoe drags

C: 1. Toe-drag 2. Short quick draws 3. Long to the side. 4. Deep forehand/backhand draw 5. Long draw back to starting position.

Stickhandling and fakes on a small surface

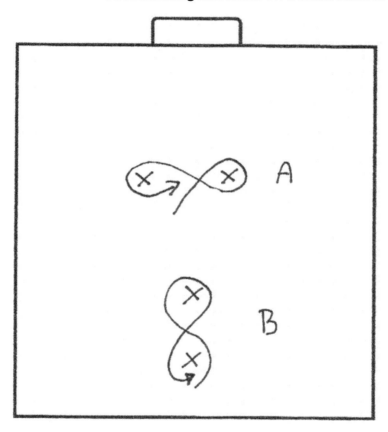

A: Dribble in an 8th sideways.

B: Dribble in an 8th in depth.

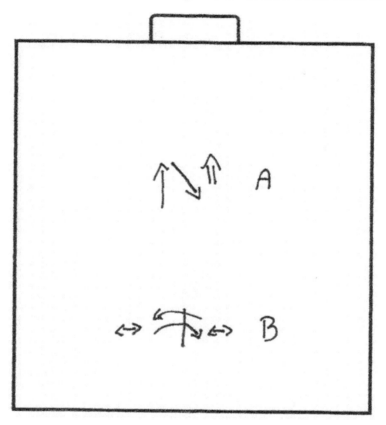

A: Backhand pull or toe drag fake and shot. Or repeat the fake over and over again.

B: Flip the ball over the obstacle, a few short quick draws on the side before flipping over the ball again.

Stickhandling and fakes on a small surface

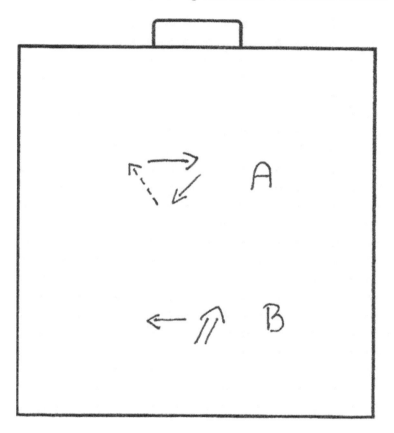

A: Pass-fake, pull aside (work with the blade, hands and body, to get the fake convincing).

B: Shot fake and sideways movement, exaggerating the shot movement so that the opponent really is convinced a shot is coming. Move the ball aside with forehand or to the other side with a backhand toe drag.

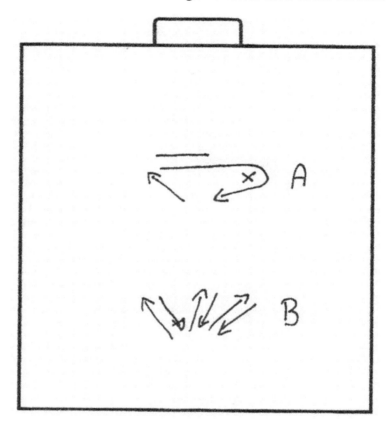

A: Move the ball toward the end of the obstacle, then a long sideways pull, around the cone.

B: Toe-drags at different angles.

Stickhandling and fakes on a small surface

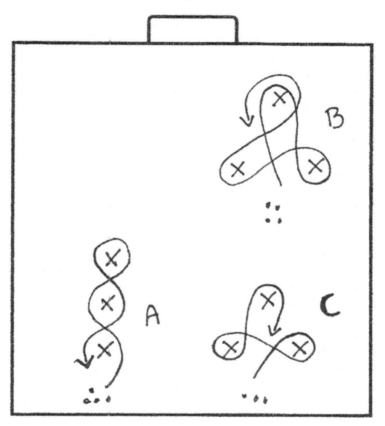

A: Slalom forward and backward with ball.

B: Dribbling around cones in triangle format.

C: Full lap around the nearest cones, long draw around the cone at the front, toe drag back.

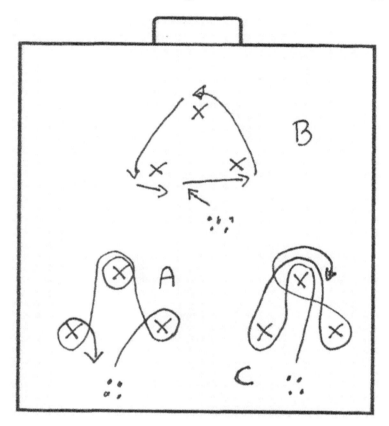

A: Full lap around all the cones.

B: Backhand toe drag to the side, backhand forward to the front cone, toe drag back to the starting position.

C: Long draws around the cones in one big unified motion.

Stickhandling and fakes on a small surface

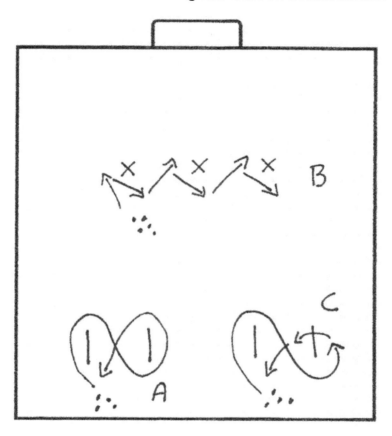

A: Longer draws in an 8th round shafts.

B: Toe drags or backhand toe drags between the cones.

C: Same as A, but you can flip the ball over one shaft or why not try flipping it over both.

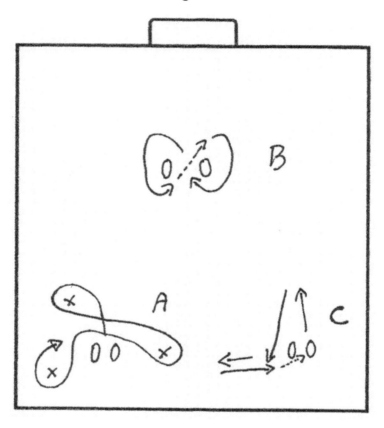

A: Around the cone diagonally in front of you, around the cone behind you to the right, the ball close to your feet and down around the left cone behind you.

B: Dribble an 8th around your own feet's.

C: Move the ball straight forward, toe-drag down, forehand out, toe-drag in and kick the ball forward with your feet.

Stickhandling and fakes on a small surface

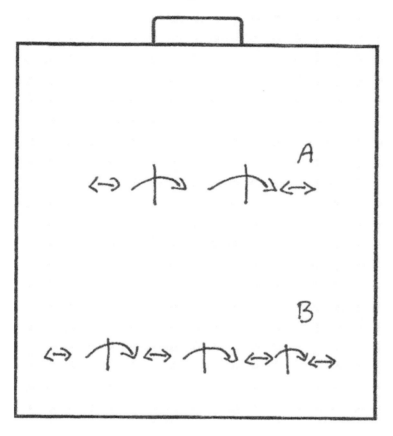

A: Dribble the ball on the left side of the first obstacle, flip over and try to flip over the next also without dribbling in the middle, dribbling on the right, before attempting to flip the ball back to the starting position.

B: Flip the ball over the obstacles and dribble short quick between each obstacle, before the next "flip".

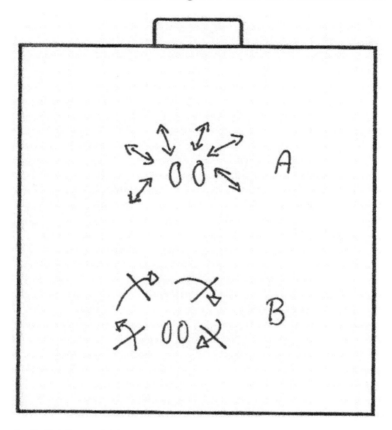

A: Dribble in different positions around your body.

B: Flip the ball over the obstacles that are around you.

Stickhandling and fakes on a small surface

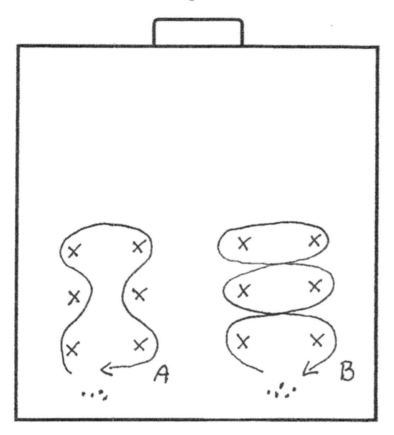

A: Slalom forward and backward.

B: Slalom forward and backward with long draws.

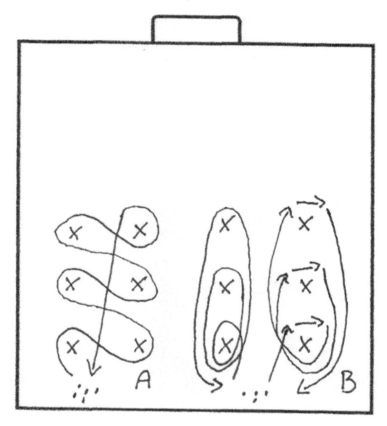

A: Slalom forward and with a long toe drag back.

B: Move the ball forward with the backhand, toe drag back (left). Same on principle on the right, but backhand toe drag past the cone.

Stickhandling and fakes on a small surface

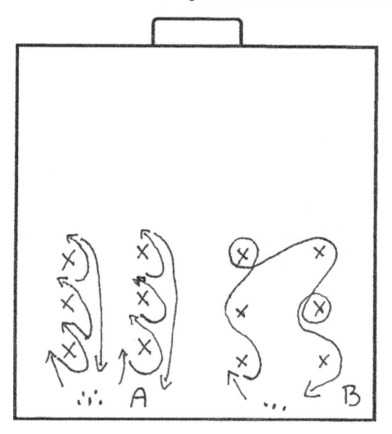

A: Backhand pull or toe drag.

B: backhand pull or toe drag at the first cone, past the next cone, full lap around the last cone on the left side. Return to the starting position using the cones on the right.

Stickhandling and fakes on a small surface

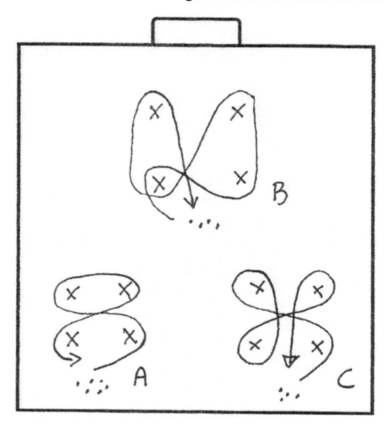

A: Longer lateral draws in sweeping motion.

B: Long draws in depth, butterfly.

C: Four clover.

Stickhandling and fakes on a small surface

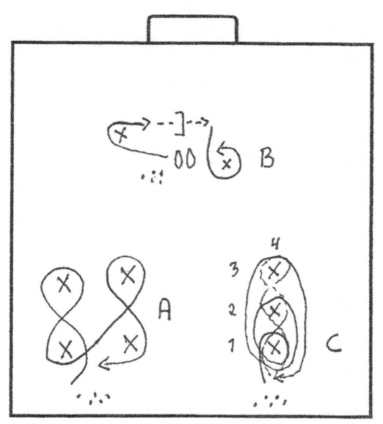

A: Dribble an 8th in depth.
B: Move the ball around the cone to the left, under the obstacle and around the cone to the right of you and back to the starting position close to the feet's.
C: 1. Ball around the nearest cone and back. 2. & 3. Ball around the next cones and back. 4. Finish with slalom straight forward and back.

Stickhandling and fakes on a small surface

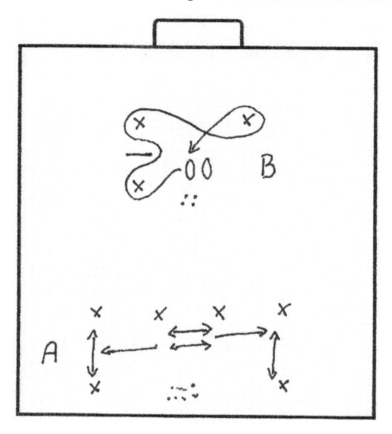

A: Dribble short fast straight in front of you, long out, and back to center, dribble straight in front, far out in the other direction, at the next turn to the side, where you also take the ball backwards.

B: Move the ball around the cone behind you, past the obstacle and the cone, over on the other side and diagonally back to the starting position.

Stickhandling and fakes on a small surface

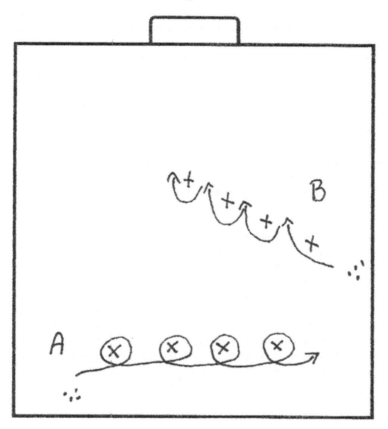

A: Full lap around the cones sideways.

B: Move the ball diagonally sideways, fake shot or pass between the cones.

Drills with ball passer

Drills with ball passer

Drills with ball passer are perfect for practicing e.g. direct shots, deliver a precise pass and to practice on pass reception. (Ball passer, plank or a car tire)

How many passes can you deliver and receive in 30 seconds?

Are you able to shoot wherever you want, even though you shoot a direct shot?

How many direct shots can you put in a predetermined spot in the goal or how many balls do you need to hit 5 times with direct shots in a predefined area?

If you do not have a ball passer, ask a parent, sibling or a friend to act as a passer.

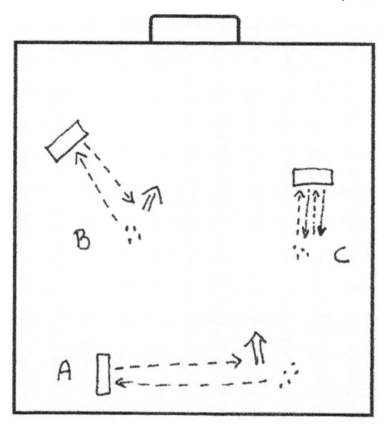

A: Stand straight against the passer and deliver a pass, direct shot.

B: Pass diagonally and shoot direct shot.

C: Stand and practice passes and pass receptions at different distances from the ball passer.

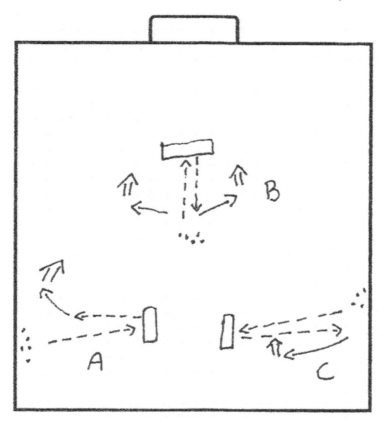

A: Pass, receive and rotate the body before the shot.

B: Pass, receive and move the ball aside before shooting.

C: Pass, receive and move the ball in the direction of the pass before shooting.

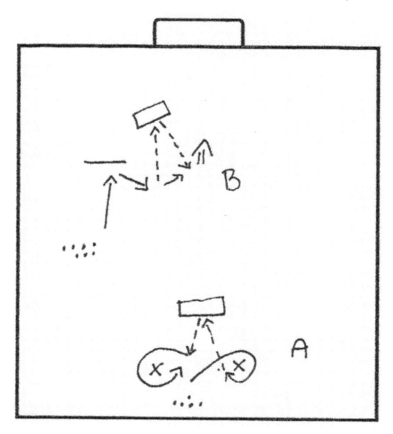

A: Dribble in an 8th, where you pass between the cones.

B: Move the ball toward the obstacle, move sideways (normal sideways draw, backhand pull or toe drag), pass and shoot direct shot.

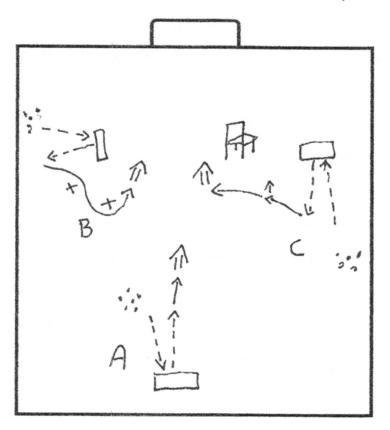

A: Stand in front of the passer and pass backwards, receive the ball and shoot quickly.

B: Pass, receive pass, dribble the cones and shoot.

C: Pass, receive pass, shot fake, past the chair before shooting or shoot low between the chair legs.

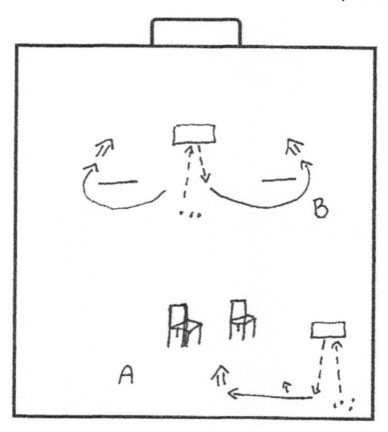

A: Pass, receive pass, shot fake, and shoot between chairs / obstacles.

B: Pass, receive pass, and move around the obstacles before shooting (you can practice protecting the ball at the shaft).

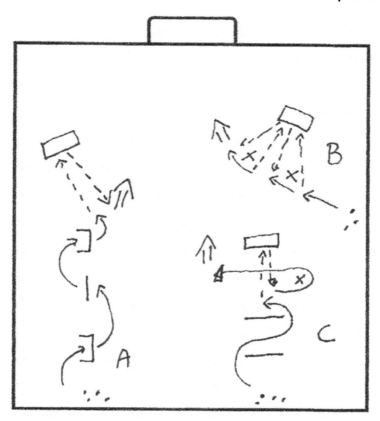

A: Jump over the obstacle, flip the ball over the next obstacle, jump, pass and shoot direct shot.

B: Move the ball forward, pass before both cones (give and go), shot.

C: Long draws between the shafts, pass, receive the ball and move it around the cone and laterally before shooting.

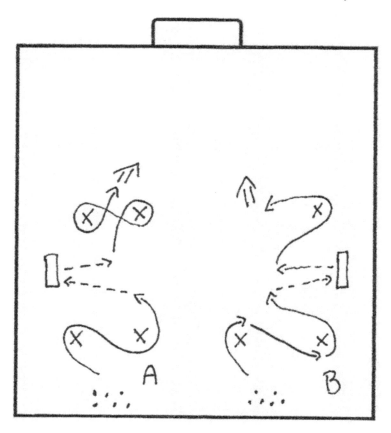

A: Move the ball around the cones, pass and receive. Full lap around the next two cones before shooting.

B: Forward towards the first cone, backhand toe drag between the cones, pass, receive and around the cone before shooting.

Drills with jumps and steps

Drills with jumps and steps

Drills with jumps are good because you work with physics and also because you might need to shoot in a position that is not completely comfortable, just like in a match.

Combining three steps, jumps, stickhandling and shots also provides an extra coordination challenge, both for your body and for your brain (multitasking).

These exercises with steps and jumps, can also be connect with drills in the stickhandling on a small surface chapter.

The exercises can also be done as solely footwork and you shoot a ball from the "pile" when you have done the steps or jumps.

Perhaps the best thing is to have the ball with you and dribble while working with your feet and end with a shot.

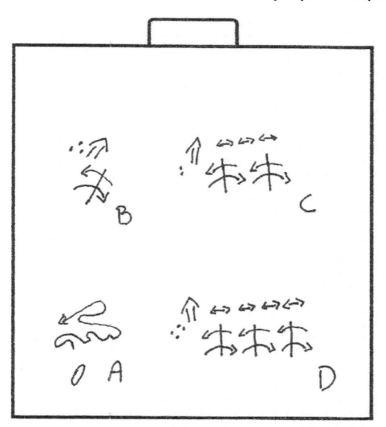

A: Jump on one leg and dribble at the same time.
B: Jumping over an obstacle back and forth (or crossover running), while dribbling a ball, or taking a shot after finishing the footwork.
C: Crossover running over two obstacles.
D: Crossover running over three obstacles

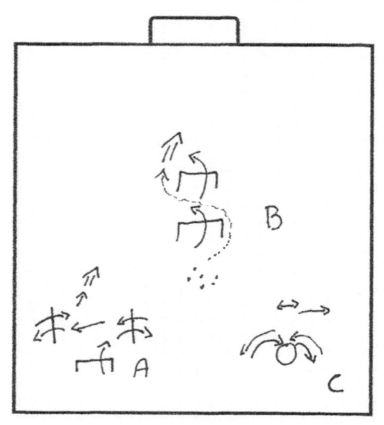

A: Jump over the first obstacle forward, and over the two obstacles on the sides in any order, shoot.

B: Jump over the obstacles, the ball goes slalom between, shoot.

C: Start with one foot on a medicine ball / soccer ball, move up the other foot on the ball, while moving down the first foot on the other side. Repeat in high speed.

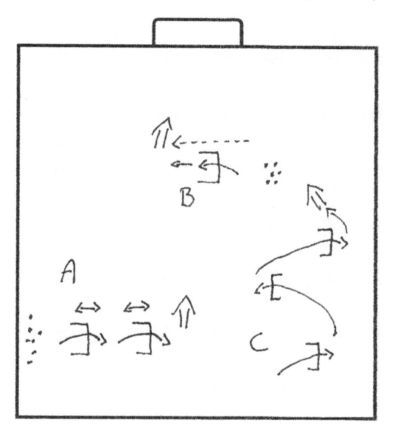

A: Jump over the obstacles sideways, finish with shot.

B: Jump over the obstacle sideways, finish with shot.

C: Jump over the obstacles, ball in front, finish with shot.

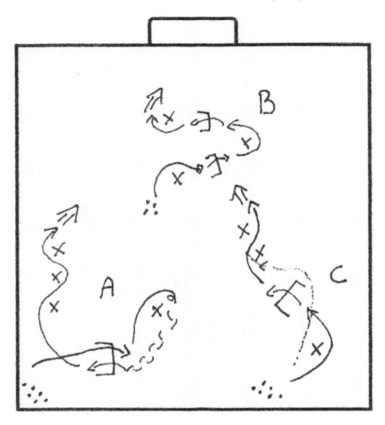

A: Jump over the obstacle sideways, around the cone, backwards towards the obstacle, jump. Dribble the cones and finish with shot.

B: Dribble the cones, jump over obstacles.

C: The body around the cone on one side, the ball on the other, jump over the obstacle, ball on the side, slalom and shot.

Odd shots, fakes and other training tips

Odd shots, fakes and other training tips

These are the shots that end up on Instagram and highlights if you score on them. However, this is just a little extra spice to the practice, things that can sometimes work on training and matches, but which you should definitely not have as your "main number".

It can be quite frustrating to see a friend try to "Zorro / Lacrosse" or shoot between the legs for the fifth time during the same match, when the teammates are free and in good goal scoring spots.

It is important to keep in mind that floorball is a team game, but at some point the perfect opportunity will emerge and then at least you are ready to take it.

However, many of these elements are good training for both mobility and skills in general, it will be easier to carry out other basic steps if you fix these odd shots or techniques as well.

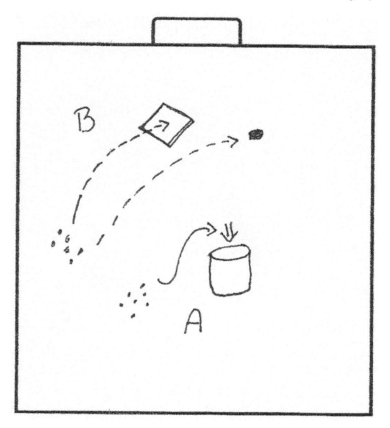

A: Flip up the ball and knock it into the bucket. Or try to "Zorro / Lacrosse" the balls in to the bucket.

B: Passing skill - try to saucer pass the ball into the wooden frame or hit another ball / puck / cone with a saucer pass. What a master you will be on saucer passes with this exercise.

Practice picking up the ball from the ground. Pull the ball back and tilt the blade under and pick up the ball on the blade. Balance the ball on the blade on the spot and

then moving around.

If you fix this more stationary on the spot, the next step is to try to make it on the move, to be able to score a "Zorro / Lacrosse goal". Move the goal forward and try get the ball in the goal with the Zorro move, starting the move behind the goal.

Juggle with the ball on the blade, practice picking up the ball from the ground.

Juggle with the blade in different angles (try the top of the blade the narrow part) or with the shaft, are you able to rotate the stick between the juggles or making a circle around the ball while it is in the air?

This is a great hand eye coordination practice.

Ask someone to throw balls at you and shoot at bouncing balls or even on volley. Or you do as in the picture, pick up the ball on the blade, throw it up and hit it on the volley.

All passes will not come perfectly during a match or training and sometimes you need to hit a bouncing ball or a ball in the air, if you fix it, it is no problem to hit the ball on the good passes either, you have trained up your hand - eye - coordination.

Approach the goal from the side or straight ahead and shoot the ball between the legs.

If you come from the side, try to get the goalkeeper in sideways movement before you shoot in the corner the goalkeeper moves from (the side you are coming in from).

If the previous variant was a bit basic and might be considered "old", then this variant is much more difficult to perform, but also more surprising for the goalkeepers.

When coming from the side, wait out the goalkeeper so that he / she must move sideways before shooting behind your back in the corner the goalkeeper moves from (the side you are coming in from).

The movement requires a lot of agility and mobility in the shoulders and arms.

If we take the example with the shot between the legs, then the goalkeepers start to be prepared for it to come and also get better at saving that shot.

Therefore, it becomes a perfect part of a fake!

Pull the ball between the legs and make the goalkeeper react and think you will shoot a shot between the legs, but instead of shooting, push the ball forward and pop it up in the net roof with a backhand.

A development of this trick could be to finish with the shot behind the back, as on the previous page, instead of shooting a backhand. Will you manage it?

If you have a ball passer, you can also use it to practice on trickier shots, such as shots between the legs, in addition to the regular direct shots (corresponds to a hard board bounce, rebound, or a pass in a real situation).

In addition to this shot being unexpected for the goalkeeper, it will also be a surprise for the defender, who will defend in front of you with the stick, blade and body, but you let the ball pass you, and put it in goal!

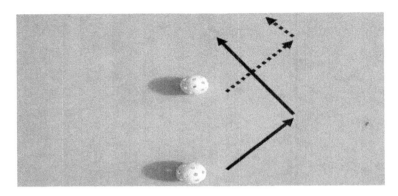

"Multitasking" - doing many things at once, or keeping track of many things at the same time, is very important and a big part of today's floorball.

A good exercise for this is to handle two or three balls, move the nearest ball aside and then past the next ball, repeating the same movement with the next ball, when the surface runs out, do it backwards back.

To add one more step, you can work with crossover running at the spot or at the same time as you move forward.

In addition, without the extra ball, this is a perfect "no touch / no move" fake on the goalkeeper. You have good speed on the ball and make the next move, the goalkeeper reacts on it and the ball slides into the goal, without you touching it at the end... this happens in best cases and if you make the move convincing.

The chair has previously been included as a "defender" in the shooting exercises, which you can shoot past, or between the legs on.

But of course it is also perfect for practicing tricks, fakes and for putting the ball between the legs on. (Or to practice poking the ball between the stick and the feet's, like a real opponent.)

Just remember, not to take the nice kitchen chair for this exercise!

Do you want to practice putting the ball under the opponent's stick or flip over?

Then you can easily build an obstacle with a small piece of the shaft from a broken hockey stick / piece of wood, which you tilt up from the ground with a few pucks or wooden blocks.

Now you have the perfect fake opponent to practice your new fakes!

Place cones and shafts around and create a creative surface to practice new things on.

Physical and Coordination training at home

- Put together your own practice

Physical and Coordination training at home

The exercises that follow now are completely without weights, besides your own body weight, or resistance from a friend in the last exercises, of course you can add on extra weights on many of the exercises, but they work just as well without. If you use weights, be sure to start calm and focus on the right technique.

You can use the exercises indoors in your room, outdoors, yourself, or in pairs.

An easy way to put together your own workout is to choose 5–6 exercises and run these 6–10 repetitions (repetitions - how many times you do it) and run 3–5 sets (set - how many times you repeat the same exercise).

To run through a program of 5-6 exercises, 6–10 repetitions and 3–5 sets take approx. 30 minutes to complete and can be done every day, you have time with that, right?

You can also set up the workouts so that you run your upper body one day (arms, stomach and back) and lower body (different leg exercises) the next day or that you mix in some of the physical exercises when you do shot and skill training, like mentioned earlier.

A coordination exercise can be included as a warm-up exercise in each workout.

Coordination exercises

Coordination - Left arm - right foot, right arm - left foot on the front

Stand still or run forward / backward

Coordination - Left arm - right foot, right arm - left foot behind the back.

Stand still or run forward / backward.

Coordination - Left arm - right foot, right arm - left foot on the front and similarly behind the back.

Stand still or run forward / backward.

Coordination - Running with high knee lifts.

You can also do heel kicks towards your buttocks.

Or do like in the previous example, mix high knees with buttocks kicks.

Stand still or run forward / backward.

Coordination - Indian dance, left arm - right foot, right arm - left foot jumping running.

Stand still, move forward or backwards.

Exercises for legs

Legs - Equal foot jump up.

Can also be performed on one leg.

Legs – Equal foot jump up, pull up the knees towards the chest (closer than the picture shows)

Can also be performed on one leg.

Legs – Sideway jumping.

Legs - Single-leg jump with knee pull towards chest, movement with side forward.

Try standing still first.

Vary the jumps with the jump leg front or behind. (In the picture, the jumping foot is "behind")

Legs - Even feet jump

Legs - Scissor Jump. Low starting position with right / left foot in front, jump and scissor the feet's in the air, land with the same foot in front as you started with.

Do series of jumps where you vary the foot that is in front (left / right)

Legs - One-Foot jump forward

Try also zigzag and backwards.

Legs and upper body - "Burbees" Start as the picture shows, jump up, land, move the legs out so that you are in a push-up position, move the legs back into the starting position in one motion.

Add push-ups to the exercise.

Legs – Jumping with both feet's sideways, locked hands.

Legs - Walking with squats, or do it standing still.

Legs - Squat on one leg with or without balance support.

Legs - Squat on one leg without support for balance, the other leg straight forward without touching the ground.

Legs - Hip lift

Legs – "Toe pull-ups", sinking deep and lifting your toes as high as possible.

Exercises for the upper body

Stomach - Feet up from the ground, moving them to the left, up, middle, up and right without touching the ground.

Stomach - Sit-ups. Feet on an imagined bench.

Vary the stop position between, high - middle - low.

Stomach - sit-ups. Feet straight up

Arms – Push-ups - wide (affects more the chest area)

Arms – Push-ups – normal

Arms – Push-ups – narrow (affects more the back of the arms – triceps)

Arms and Legs – Push-up (1-8), running forward with four-wheel drive (hands and feet on the ground), four steps, repeat the same.

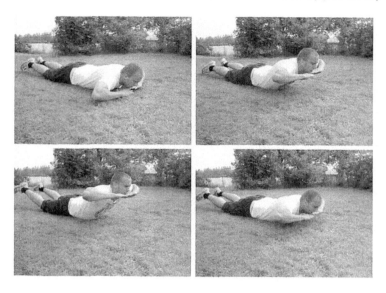

Back - Back lift.

Back - Back Exercise - Lift the right arm and left foot and the opposite next time.

Fun physical exercises in pairs

Strength - Start in wheelbarrow position. Release one leg, the other tries to hold the leg upright. Repeat with the other leg. Drop right - left at the beginning, random after that. You can add push-ups to the exercise.

Strength - Start in reverse wheelbarrow position.
Release one leg, the other tries to hold the leg upright.
Repeat with the other leg. Drop right - left at the
beginning, random after that. You can add triceps push-
ups to the exercise.

Strength - Start in wheelbarrow position. Pull the buddy back as far as possible and then back to the starting position.

You can add push-ups to the exercise.

Strength - Start in wheelbarrow position. Push the buddy forward as far as possible and then back to the starting position.

You can add push-ups to the exercise.

Fun physical exercises in pairs

Strength - The feet rise from the ground, moving them in circles without touching the buddy's feet or the ground.

Strength - Wrestling on the knees.

Fun physical exercises in pairs

Strength – Push-up position, try to bring down the other.

Legs - Squats in pairs. Hook your arms and start doing squats in pairs.

Legs - Squats in pairs. One is on the buddy's shoe soles when he does squats.

Legs - Catapult squats in pairs. One sits on the buddy's shoe soles, which makes a squat and pushes away his friend.

Fun physical exercises in pairs

Legs - The one lying down bends the legs up and the other slows down (brakes) the movement. Then the one "sitting down" presses the other ones feet to the ground, while the he try to slowdown the movement.

Leg - Shoulder to shoulder in pairs, try to get across to the companion's side of a thought line or a real line, while the pair moves forward.

Legs - Grab each other's hands, try to get over the companion on your side of a thought line or a real line, while moving forward sideways.

Legs - One pulls and the other brakes while the pair moves straight back.

Legs - The one in front brakes and the one behind pushes the other one forward.

Legs - "Leg wrestling" Lie down with your feet in the opposite direction, lift the foot closest to your buddy and try to break it down to the ground.

Legs - Squat, try to push the other one down with your hands.

Strength and balance - Try to get your buddy to move their feet and get out of balance.

Strength and balance - Try dragging your buddy to your side of the line.

Have fun - Practice for your own sake!

Have fun - Practice for your own sake!

You are the one playing floorball and a lot of the feeling, how fun something is, will be about how much you have trained, the more you train, the better you will become and be able to do things better than others, which will make it fun, you succeed!

The same principle applies to floorball, other sports or school, invest your time in training!

Remember that in all training you need to see things on long term, you are not an app or figure in a game, which can be upgraded with a "touch", it takes a lot of work for a long time to succeed and almost every day if you want to become "best". Everything you do now you have with you!

Make the training a daily good habit, which you do in the long term, you will not be the best, because you train today and not because you train tomorrow, but because you can manage to keep the training over time and have it as a "daily good habit" or at least an often recurring good habit during the weeks, to train yourself (in addition to the team training). You will surely see results and feel that what you are doing is fun!

Train hard and often, I believe in you!

Challenge tables

100 Day Challenge

Activity:

1	2	3	4	5	6	7	8	9	10
11	12	13	14	15	16	17	18	19	20
21	22	23	24	25	26	27	28	29	30
31	32	33	34	35	36	37	38	39	40
41	42	43	44	45	46	47	48	49	50
51	52	53	54	55	56	57	58	59	60
61	62	63	64	65	66	67	68	69	70
71	72	73	74	75	76	77	78	79	80
81	82	83	84	85	86	87	88	89	90
91	92	93	94	95	96	97	98	99	100

Decide on an activity and write it, then tick a box every time you complete the activity 100 times. Tick until you reach 100 crosses or in other words 100 days. Then you have trained 10,000 times on e.g. shots or a certain fake.

100 Day Challenge

Activity:

1	2	3	4	5	6	7	8	9	10
11	12	13	14	15	16	17	18	19	20
21	22	23	24	25	26	27	28	29	30
31	32	33	34	35	36	37	38	39	40
41	42	43	44	45	46	47	48	49	50
51	52	53	54	55	56	57	58	59	60
61	62	63	64	65	66	67	68	69	70
71	72	73	74	75	76	77	78	79	80
81	82	83	84	85	86	87	88	89	90
91	92	93	94	95	96	97	98	99	100

Decide on an activity and write it, then tick a box every time you complete the activity 100 times. Tick until you reach 100 crosses or in other words 100 days. Then you have trained 10,000 times on e.g. shots or a certain fake.

100 Day Challenge

Activity:

1	2	3	4	5	6	7	8	9	10
11	12	13	14	15	16	17	18	19	20
21	22	23	24	25	26	27	28	29	30
31	32	33	34	35	36	37	38	39	40
41	42	43	44	45	46	47	48	49	50
51	52	53	54	55	56	57	58	59	60
61	62	63	64	65	66	67	68	69	70
71	72	73	74	75	76	77	78	79	80
81	82	83	84	85	86	87	88	89	90
91	92	93	94	95	96	97	98	99	100

Decide on an activity and write it, then tick a box every time you complete the activity 100 times. Tick until you reach 100 crosses or in other words 100 days. Then you have trained 10,000 times on e.g. shots or a certain fake.

Training weeks

Target: I will practice _____ times per week, for _____ minutes

1	2	3	4	5	6	7	8	9	10
11	12	13	14	15	16	17	18	19	20
21	22	23	24	25	26	27	28	29	30
31	32	33	34	35	36	37	38	39	40
41	42	43	44	45	46	47	48	49	50
51	52								

Set a goal for yourself, how many times you should train yourself (extra at home) each week and for how long. When you have done it during the week, you get to cross over the week.

Training weeks

Target: I will practice _____ times per week, for _____ minutes

1	2	3	4	5	6	7	8	9	10
11	12	13	14	15	16	17	18	19	20
21	22	23	24	25	26	27	28	29	30
31	32	33	34	35	36	37	38	39	40
41	42	43	44	45	46	47	48	49	50
51	52								

Set a goal for yourself, how many times you should train yourself (extra at home) each week and for how long. When you have done it during the week, you get to cross over the week.

My personal best		
Activity (what was the challenge)	Record (Nbr of times or time)	When (date)

Write the activity, e.g. number of laps in an 8th, in 30 seconds, the record and date. *See pages 49-50.*

My personal best		
Activity (what was the challenge)	Record (Nbr of times or time)	When (date)

Write the activity, e.g. number of laps in an 8th, in 30 seconds, the record and date. *See pages 49-50.*

Follow us on:

@Flrballcom

Flrball.com